YOUR STORY

YOUR FOREVER FAMILY

Love You Forever …

Love Makes A Family

A LITTLE MESSAGE TO SAY HOW MUCH WE LOVE YOU....

ALL ABOUT _____
You Grew In My Heart…

FULL NAME: _____   BIRTHDAY: _____

WHERE I GREW UP:

MY BEST CHILDHOOD MEMORIES:

MY INTERESTS & HOBBIES:

WHAT I WANT YOU TO KNOW ABOUT ME:

My Love Letter To You:

_____

_____

_____

_____

_____

_____

_____

_____

NEVER FORGET…

MY DREAM FOR YOU…

ALL ABOUT _____

Love To Make Memories With You…

FULL NAME: BIRTHDAY:

WHERE I GREW UP:

MY BEST CHILDHOOD MEMORIES:

MY INTERESTS & HOBBIES:

WHAT I WANT YOU TO KNOW ABOUT ME:

My Love Letter To You:

_____

_____

_____

_____

_____

_____

_____

NEVER FORGET...

MY DREAM FOR YOU...

ALL ABOUT YOU

FULL NAME: BIRTHDAY:

THE FIRST DAY WE MET!
A Day I Will Never Forget!

How I Felt:

What Happened?

When You Came Home:

SOME FIRSTS…
You Bring So Much Joy Into My Life!

☆

☆

☆

MY HOPES AND DREAMS FOR YOU BY _____

MY HOPES AND DREAMS FOR YOU BY _____

THE BEST MEMORIES EVER!

ALL YOU
need
IS
love

WATCHING YOU GROW...

Notes:

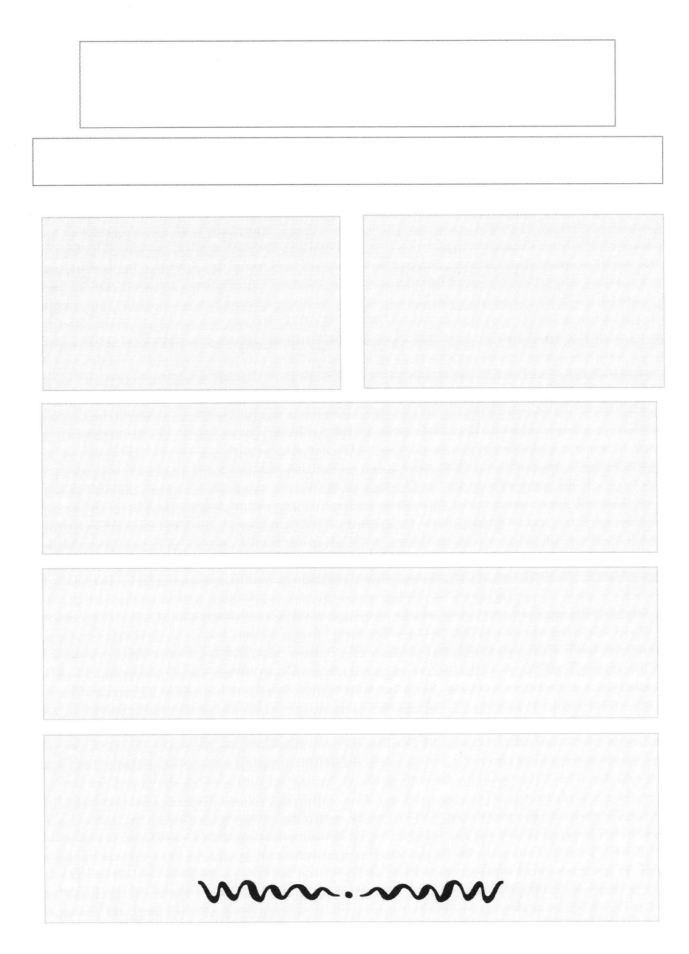

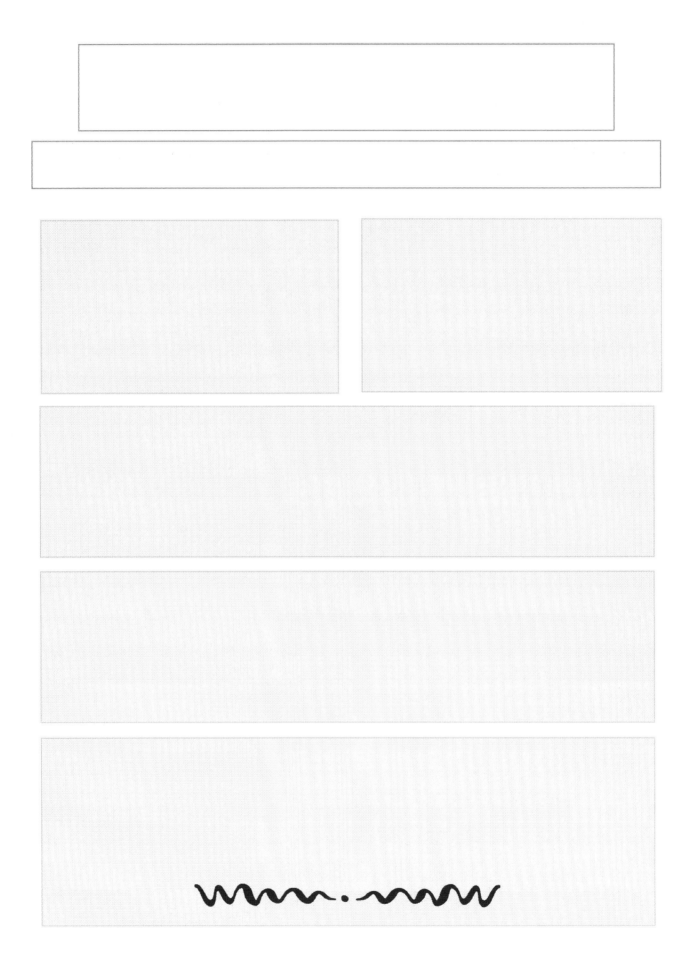

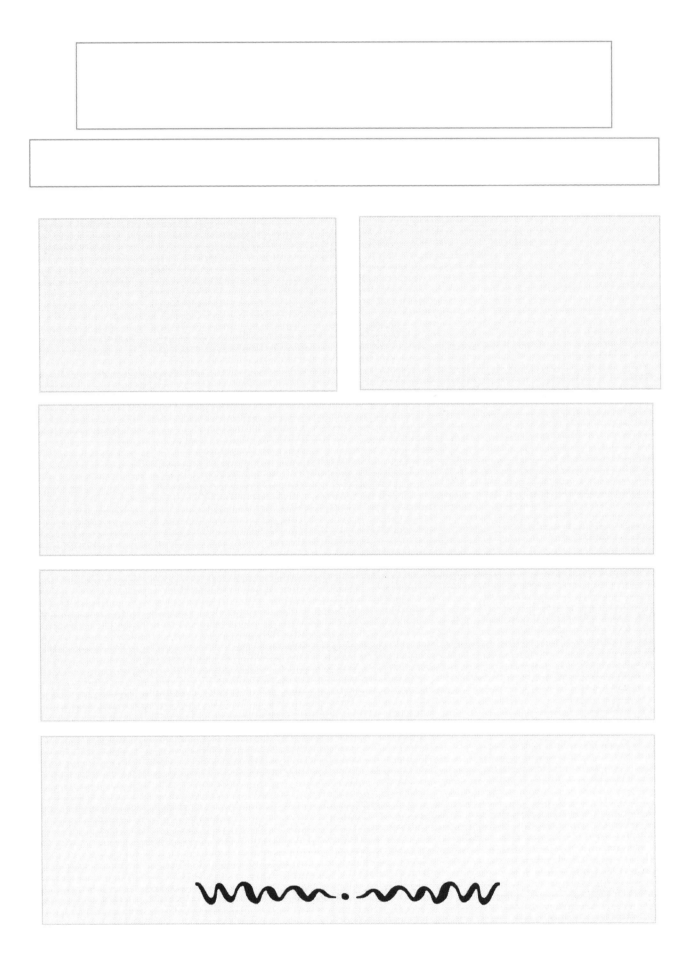

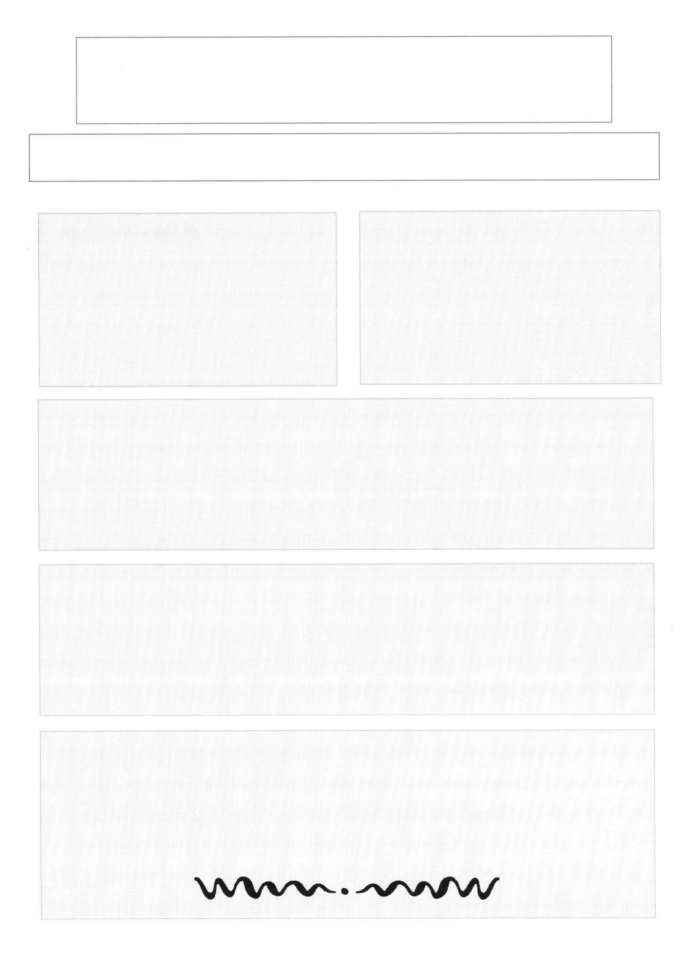

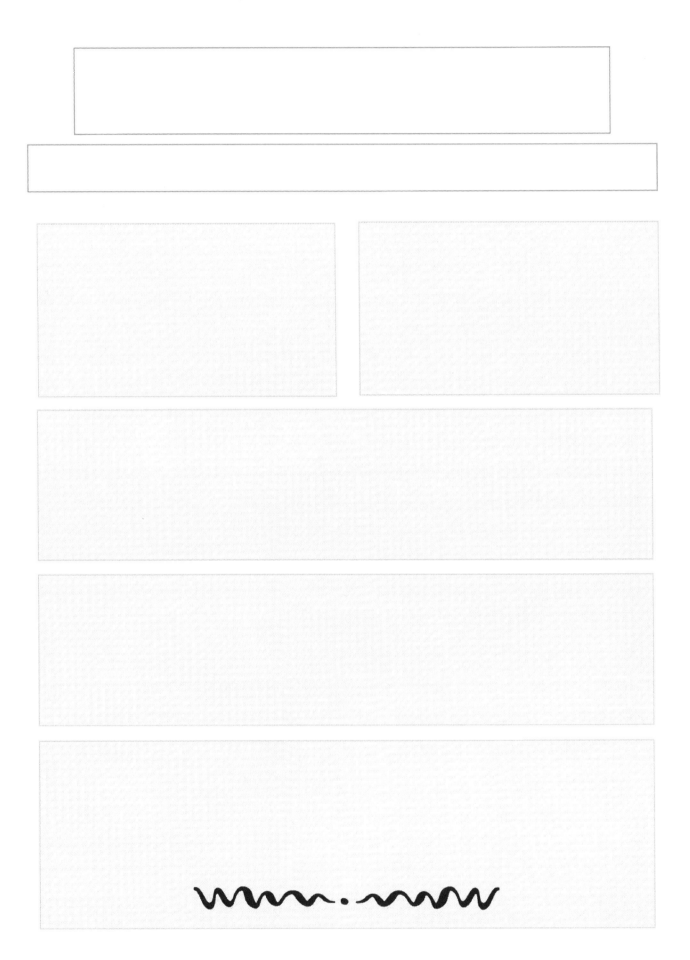

www.www

www.mww

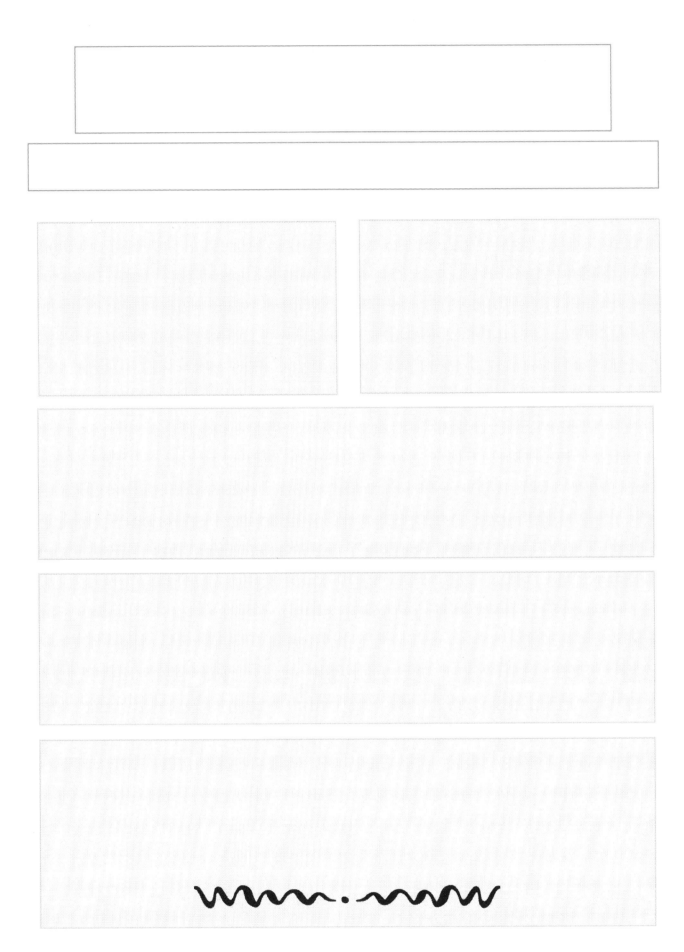

www.mww

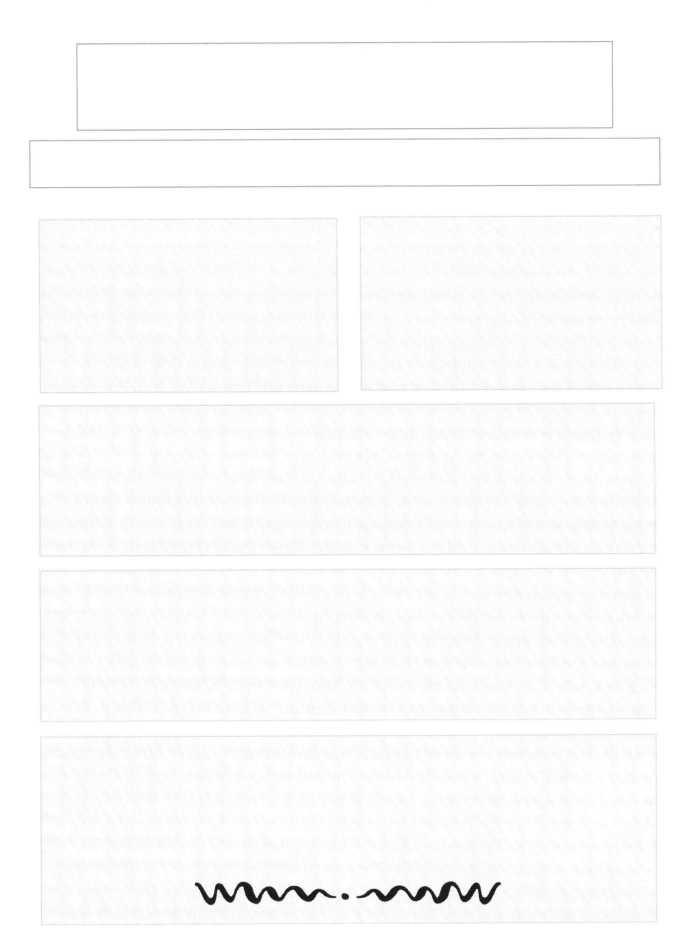

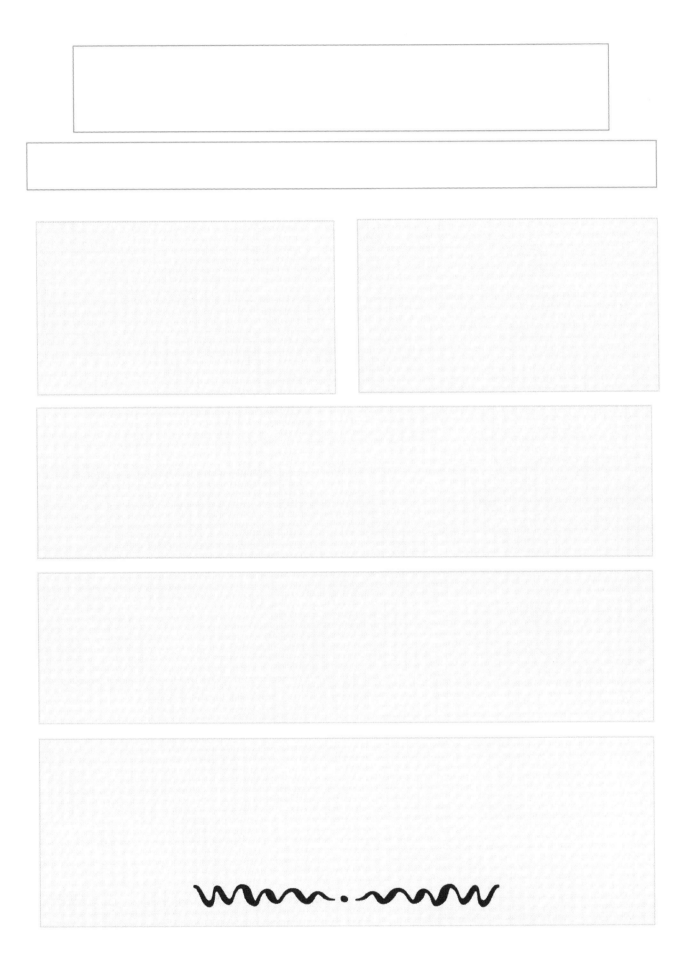

Forever Grateful

Made in the USA
Middletown, DE
14 December 2021